PANTRY MAGIC

Making and Using

Fruit and Vegetable Powders

By
Elaine Broughton

elaineinthekitchen.com

Published in 2017 by Elaine in the Kitchen
17 126th Lane NW
P.O. Box 48121
Coon Rapids, MN 55448

Copyright © 2017 by Elaine Broughton
All rights reserved. No part of this publication may be reproduced, distributed, or transmitted in any form or by any means, including photocopying, recording or other electronic or mechanical methods, without the prior written permission of the publisher, except in the case of brief quotations embodied in critical reviews and certain other noncommercial uses permitted by copyright law.

ISBN: 978-0-9983717-0-2
ISBN: 978-0-9983717-1-9

Cover design by Elaine Broughton

For Lisa who is my constant inspiration.

ACKNOWLEDGEMENTS

It's been said that there is no new thing under the sun, and thus I acknowledge that I did not invent anything in this book. The techniques for drying fruits and vegetables have been used for thousands of years. I used many sources in preparing this book and hopefully, others will find the information useful and pass that knowledge on to others. I'd like to thank all of the grandmothers, grandfathers, homesteaders, farm families, bloggers, preppers and others who have shared with all of us their knowledge of the techniques for drying and storing food.

And special thanks to Mary Lynn Lewis, writer, editor and friend for her advice and unerring eye in helping proof this book.

Table of Secrets

INTRODUCTION 1
BROCCOLI POWDER 9
CABBAGE POWDER 13
CARROT POWDER 15
CELERY POWDER 19
CUCUMBER POWDER 21
JALAPENO POWDER 23
MUSHROOM POWDER 25
PUMPKIN POWDER 29
SUPER GREEN POWDER 33
SWEET POTATO POWDER 37
TOMATO POWDER 41
FRUIT POWDERS 47
APPLE POWDER 49
BANANA POWDER 51
BLACKBERRY/RASPBERRY POWDER 53
BLUEBERRY POWDER 55
CITRUS POWDERS 57
CRANBERRY POWDER 61
STRAWBERRY POWDER 63
THOUGHTS FROM THE AUTHOR 65
RECIPE INDEX 67

v

INTRODUCTION

We all have secrets, even in the kitchen. Every pantry needs a store of secret ingredients that can make everyday kitchen creations not just mysteriously delicious but wonderfully healthy and nutritious. Fruit and vegetable powders are a great way to do just that because drying and powdering foods greatly concentrates their flavor and nutritional qualities.

A little creativity can save you money, make you a better cook and bring gourmet quality flavors to your table. This book will show you how to create mealtime magic by making your own secret ingredients using flavoring elements, and shortcut ingredients that are made from food items we normally have in our refrigerator or pantry. You can create and use powders to help make your meals healthier, tastier, easier to prepare, and at the same time keep unused food from going to waste.

Very few of us get the amount of fruits and vegetables that we should and let's face it, every family has someone in the house who simply hates vegetables or an ingredient that's needed to make a particular dish special. It may be an allergy, a texture that they just can't stand or maybe they refuse to eat vegetables because they were frightened by Brussel sprouts as a child. Still, those of us who love mushrooms shouldn't have to give up eating them, or be forced to cook two separate meals to keep everyone happy.

The purpose of this book is to show you how to make a mushroom hater love that earthy yumminess without actually having to put one in their mouth, and how you can put some extra nutrition into everything from spaghetti sauce to baked potatoes. Brighten desserts, sauces and soups using secret ingredients like citrus or celery powder, and do it all without resorting to manufactured flavorings and extracts.

Best of all, you will learn how to save money, prep time, and storage space using shelf stable powders stored in your pantry.

Welcome to cooking with vegetable and fruit powders.

Basic Dehydration and Powder Making

There are a few basic tools you will need to make vegetable and fruit powders:

- Dehydrator or racks for drying
- Glass jars with lids for storage
- Dedicated spice or coffee grinder
- Small sieve or mesh strainer
- Food brush
- Labels

You could also use your oven, although the lowest temperature in most ovens is still too high to preserve color and nutritional value, but the oven will work for some fruits and vegetables such as tomatoes.

For foods like lemon, lime or orange peel, air drying works really well. Simply place the peeled zest in a dish and set it on the counter in a dry warm spot. You can also make an air drying tray by using two (new) window screens or stretching window screening material over two frames and placing the fruits or vegetables between the two layers. I sometimes use extra dehydrator trays to create my own air drying trays. Just load the trays up and set in a dry, well ventilated spot. I don't recommend doing this outside since it encourages scavenging by a variety of curious, hungry creatures (like squirrels, children and husbands). Some resourceful souls put the trays in the car with the windows rolled up. Careful with the onions or garlic since the smell is strong and will linger. You can also use the pulp from juicing, dehydrate it and grind into powder.

Powdering Equipment

Coffee grinders are very inexpensive, about $15-$20 at Walmart or Target. I recommend that you have a grinder that is used only for powdering or grinding dried vegetables and fruits. The faint taste of coffee can be a little off-putting in a bowl of mashed carrots, and garlic in your morning coffee is just unacceptable.

I think glass jars are best for storage because they can be sterilized and sealed. I use canning jars but other glass food containers can be used. Just be careful how you clean them and make sure the lids are tight fitting.

You'll need a small sieve or strainer and a brush to empty the grinder.

Label your jars with the name and date of the ingredients.

Technique

Not all powders are created in the same way. Different fruits and vegetables may require different methods.

Berries, such as blueberries and soft fruits like raspberries can be placed in the dehydrator frozen. Some people like to blend them to a paste and spread on trays. Sweet potatoes, carrots, pumpkin and butternut squash should be cooked and puree them first. Spread the puree on trays to dry and then grind to powder when the puree is fully dried.

Vegetables like celery, broccoli, mushrooms and carrots should be blanched first to preserve the color. Blanching also removes any hidden dirt or garden pests. A quick way to do this is to place the cut pieces into a bowl or plate, cover with plastic wrap and put in the microwave for about 2 minutes. Once you have completed this step, the vegetables can be dehydrated and ground.

High moisture vegetables like cucumbers can just be peeled, sliced and dehydrated, and cabbage only needs to be sliced into ribbons, rinsed and dehydrated. Both cucumbers and cabbage dehydrate and powder beautifully, especially red cabbage. Don't slice the fruits or vegetables too thin or the dried pieces may fall through the dehydrator trays or stick to the trays and you won't be able to remove them.

Citrus fruit can be zested or the peels shaved off with a vegetable peeler and then air dried, either in a bowl. This preserves the color and nutritional elements better than heat drying. However, you can use a dehydrator on a very low setting.

You can also dehydrate and powder the flesh of the fruit. Slice the peeled or zested fruit into rings and dry either by air drying, or on a low setting in the dehydrator. Grind that into powder also, separate from the zest.

Leafy herbs like mint, cilantro and watercress can be air dried for best results as well as spinach, escarole, kale and other greens. I like to remove the woody ribs in kale and collards because they don't powder well.

All temperatures listed in this book are given in Fahrenheit degrees. I don't list drying times since those can vary greatly depending on humidity and moisture in the fruit or vegetable. If it's crisp, it's dry.

Here are just a few things to keep in mind:

Think of your powders as a seasoning or condiment instead of a main ingredient. Dehydrated foods are concentrated so a pinch or spoonful is all you need.

Vegetables and fruits that have been dehydrated at home have not been fully cooked, so they will need some time to rehydrate.

Dehydrated powders aren't good for making juice. Most commercial drink powders are made from juice which has been reduced and dehydrated. Emulsifiers are then added to make them dissolve faster.

BROCCOLI POWDER

Broccoli is a major superfood. However, there are only so many ways to eat broccoli. Drying and making your own broccoli powder turns it into a secret ingredient that you can add to all kinds of dishes. It's also a great money saver because you can dehydrate and powder fresh or frozen broccoli, especially if it's on sale, for pennies.

Preparation:

If you are using frozen broccoli you will need to use about two to three 12-ounce bags and you don't need to do any blanching. However, if you use fresh broccoli (2 bundles, cut and cleaned) first soak it in salt water for about an hour to remove any debris. Then cut into bite size pieces and blanch for 2-3 minutes to preserve the color and nutrients. After blanching, chop it in the food processor for convenience in drying and grinding.

Spread the broccoli in a thin layer on the dehydrator trays. Dry until the broccoli is completely dry and you can break it into pieces.

Dehydrator Temperature: 115° - 125°

Grind the dried broccoli pieces into a fine powder, and put through a sieve. Any large pieces left over can be saved in a container to use in soups or stews. I toss all of the too large pieces from all my dried vegetables into a jar and save to use in soups.

Store the powder in an airtight glass container and use in soups, salads, smoothies, to flavor pasta, or sprinkle on baked potatoes. Mix with hot distilled water and rehydrate to make homemade baby food.

Broccoli Powder

Try this Recipe Idea:

Baked Potato with Broccoli Dust

1. Bake a large russet potato until tender. Split the potato and add a dollop or two of butter, sour cream or Greek yogurt. Sprinkle generously with broccoli powder. The broccoli powder makes a great substitute for salt and you may not even need pepper. Remember, vegetable powders are used for seasoning, not as the main ingredient.

2. Prepare <u>Creamy Soup Mix</u> (pages 45-46) as directed and add 2 tablespoons of broccoli powder. Sprinkle cheddar cheese on the top and serve.

CABBAGE

Cabbage is one of the healthiest, most nutritious vegetables on the table. It's also known for its anti-cancer properties, as a treatment for stomach ulcers and it's available year round. This makes it a great secret ingredient to add to dishes.

Preparation:

Cabbage, green and red, dries beautifully and makes a wonderful powder. Just slice and rinse the cabbage into 1 inch ribbons, spread on the dehydrator tray and dry at a low temperature. Air drying also works. Both those methods preserve the color and nutrition of the cabbage. Red cabbage in particular makes a striking deep reddish purple powder.

Dehydrator temperature: 115° - 120°

When the ribbons are dry and crispy, grind them to a fine powder. Put through a sieve and any coarse pieces can be put into the container with the other large unground vegetable pieces and saved for soups.

Cabbage powder, red or green, adds extra flavor and nutrition to your cooking. Use it in soups, smoothies, sprinkle on salads, and in many other dishes.

Try These Recipe Ideas:

Red cabbage powder can be used in making vegetable dyes.

Ulcer Healing Cabbage Smoothie
Combine 1 cup carrot juice or filtered water, 1 tablespoon red or green cabbage powder, ½ banana, ½ apple. Blend until smooth.

Secret Vegetable Soup
Add 1 or 2 tablespoons of cabbage powder, red or green, to vegetable soup, tomato soup, carrot ginger soup, broccoli cream soup or any stew. It's a great secret way to add extra vitamins and nutrients.

CARROT POWDER

Carrots are one of the tastiest and most versatile of vegetables, and carrot powder makes a great secret ingredient in all kinds of dishes.

Preparation:

Clean and peel 5 lbs. of carrots. Grate or chop by hand or in the food processor. Blanch or place on a microwave safe plate, cover with plastic wrap and heat in the microwave for 1 - 2 minutes. This also enhances the sweetness of the carrots.

Dehydrator temperature: 115° - 120°

Spread the carrots on the dehydrator trays. Let the carrots dehydrate until all the moisture is gone and the carrot pieces are crispy. Let cool and grind to a fine powder.

Sift through a fine sieve. Save any pieces that did not reduce to powder for other uses. Store in an airtight glass container.

Use for smoothies, soup, pasta, pastry, soufflé, homemade baby food, artisan soap, skin care and anything else your imagination can invent.

Try This Recipe Idea:

Easy Carrot Pudding

1 12.5 oz. package firm Silken tofu
3 teaspoons carrot powder
6 tablespoons water
¼ teaspoon ground cardamom
2 tablespoons sugar, honey, maple syrup or other sweetener

Mix the carrot powder and water and set aside to rehydrate for 15 minutes. Add 1/4 teaspoon cardamom. Then cover with plastic wrap and microwave for 1 minute.

In food processor, combine all ingredients and process until smooth. Spoon into dessert glasses and chill. Another great idea is to fill 4 oz. glass jars and put them in lunches.

This is a great high protein, low fat, vitamin packed dessert.

Carrot Cashew Hummus

¼ cup carrot powder
¾ cup hot water
½ cup raw cashews (soak for 30 minutes)

Stir hot water into the carrot powder and let sit for 10-15 minutes to rehydrate. Then, combine all ingredients in food processor or blender and blend until smooth. Add 1 tsp cumin, 1 tsp garam masala and stir. Serve as a dip or spread.

CELERY POWDER

Lots of kitchens have celery salt and celery seed, but celery powder is outstanding as a secret ingredient in many different kinds of dishes. It is an excellent substitute for salt, and the concentrated flavor adds a special something to soups, salad dressings, dips and many other dishes.

Preparation:

Thoroughly clean the celery stalks and cut into 2 inch slices. Blanch to preserve color. The slices will shrink as they dehydrate and you want them to be big enough so they don't fall through the dehydrator trays. You can also put the pieces into a food processor and then spread the shredded celery on the fruit leather trays to dry.

Dehydrator temperature: 115° - 125°

Celery Powder

When the celery is dry and crispy, grind it to a fine powder. Put the powder through a sieve, adding the big pieces left over to the jar of other vegetable discards. You should store powders in an air tight glass container.

Try This Recipe Idea:

Celery powder is an excellent salt substitute. You can use it as a seasoning in soup, salads, on baked or mashed potatoes and in any dish where you want to add extra freshness and flavor.

When serving Bloody Mary's, coat the rim of the glass in celery powder.

20

CUCUMBER POWDER

You can do a lot more with cucumbers than make pickles, and although it seems unlikely that you could dehydrate a vegetable with such a high moisture content, cucumbers actually dry very well.

Preparation:

Wash the cucumbers and slice them in 1 inch rounds, or halves. I didn't peel or remove the seeds since I was using small cucumbers from the garden. If using more mature fruits you might want to peel and remove the seeds.

Dehydrator Temperature: 115° - 120°

Cucumber Powder

When the cucumbers are crispy dry, grind them into a fine powder and put through a sieve to remove unground pieces. Store the celery powder in an airtight glass container.

Cucumber powder makes a great secret ingredient in dip, sauces, sprinkled on salad, on fresh vegetables and drinks like lemonade and fruit waters.

Try These Recipe Ideas:

I like to sprinkle cucumber powder on sliced tomatoes, or add a pinch to tzatziki or cucumber dill sauce. You can also use cucumber powder for soap making and to prepare your own facial masks and toners.

You can create a different flavor for cucumber powder by using higher drying temperature. This gives the powder a beautiful toasted flavor that's both sweet and slightly sour.

JALAPENO POWDER

Powdered jalapeno is a very popular item with online shoppers and it goes by some very colorful names like Texas Gunpowder™ and Louisiana Lightning. It's become a staple in many American kitchens and it's really easy to make.

Preparation:

Wash and slice the jalapenos and place them on the dehydrator trays. I strongly recommend that you wear gloves while slicing and handling the peppers. Wash your hands thoroughly and DO NOT TOUCH YOUR FACE OR EYES.

Dehydrator temperature: 115° - 125°

I recommend that you place the dehydrator in another room that can be closed off, or outside in a safe location. Otherwise,

Jalapeno Powder

the smell of jalapenos will permeate the house and irritate eyes and noses.

When the jalapenos are dry, grind them to a fine powder and pass through a sieve to remove any large pieces or unground seeds. Again, use caution when opening the grinder and let the powder settle for a minute or two before opening. Breathing jalapeno dust is definitely not something you want to do.

Try These Recipe Ideas:

Mix salt and jalapeno powder in a shaker, then sprinkle on dishes like nachos and cheese sauce, add to white cream gravy instead of sausage or coat the rim of your margarita glasses in jalapeno salt.

Make your own chili paste by combining 2 tablespoons of jalapeno powder with ¼ cup warm water and a drizzle of olive oil. Use is soups, stews, your favorite Asian or African dishes.

Combine jalapeno powder with salt in a shaker and sprinkle on soups or salads.

MUSHROOM POWDER

This is one of those foods that people seem to either love or hate, but regardless of how you feel about them, mushrooms are one of nature's superfoods, rich in vitamins and minerals as well as one of the best foods to improve your immune system.

Mushrooms are also one of the best secret ingredients for adding that extra depth of flavor to meats, marinades, sauces, gravies, and soups. It's a must-have in any kitchen. Mushroom powder is available online and in high end supermarkets. but it's really expensive to buy. Making it at home is a money saver, and a stealthy way to add that rich mushroom flavor without upsetting all the anti-mushroom eaters.

Mushroom Powder

Preparation:

Start with about a pound of mushrooms. Buy them on sale and pick up several boxes. I like the richer flavor of cremini (baby portabellas), but if you are fortunate enough to acquire some dried porcini or other varieties, add those to the mix for extra taste. You can use dried mushrooms in the store, but fresh ones are usually easier to find and much less expensive.

To prepare, brush the mushrooms clean and cut them in 1-2 inch slices. You could quarter them, but the slices fit better on my dehydrator trays, and dry faster than larger pieces. Put the mushrooms on a plate or dish, cover with plastic wrap and blanch them in the microwave for just about 30 seconds. Remove the plastic wrap and blot dry with a paper towel. Place the mushrooms slices on the drying tray in a single layer.

Dehydrator temperature: 115° - 120°

When completely dry (pieces should break instead of bend), grind to a fine powder. Let the powder settle. If you open it too soon you'll get a face full of mushroom dust. I like them on my food, just not in my lungs.

Try These Recipe Ideas:

Use mushroom powder in a shaker to sprinkle on any meat, fish or grilled vegetable.

Add a tablespoon of mushroom powder to give deep, rich flavors to soups, stews, sauces and gravies.

Add 1-2 tablespoons to <u>Creamy Soup Mix</u> (pages 45-46) and prepare as directed for wonderful cream of mushroom soup.

Mushroom Gravy

Prepare Creamy Soup Mix as above. You can replace the water with chicken or vegetable stock. Add 1-2 tablespoons mushroom powder and season to taste.

PUMPKIN POWDER

The Great Pumpkin is more than a clever cartoon idea. If you know how to prepare, store and use it, pumpkin truly is one of the great gifts from the garden.

Fresh pumpkin isn't difficult to find in most large supermarkets in late summer and early fall. I recommend selecting a small to medium size pumpkin depending on the amount of pumpkin powder (or flour) you want to make. A medium size pumpkin will produce up to two quart jars of powder.

Preparation:

Cut your pumpkin into halves or quarters if it is a large one. Clean the fiber from the inside of the pumpkin and save the seeds for roasting. Then place the pumpkin pieces face down in a baking sheet or roasting pan with 1-2 inches of water. Bake in a 350° oven for 1-2 hours or until a knife inserts easily.

When the pumpkin is done, remove from the oven and let cool until you can handle it easily. The rind should peel away easily, but you can also scoop out the flesh and put in a bowl. Discard the rind. I mash or puree the pulp in the food processor for more consistent drying.

Spread the pureed pulp evenly on the dehydrator trays. About an inch thickness works for me. If you don't have enough plastic tray liners, just cut sheets of parchment paper to fit the trays and use that. Another method is to shred the uncooked pumpkin or cut into cubes.

Dehydrator temperature: 115-130°

I prefer to use fresh pumpkin but if you don't have the time or space to prepare fresh pumpkin, there is commercially canned pumpkin. Sometimes there's nothing wrong with taking the easy way out. Depending on how much pumpkin powder you want to keep on hand, a couple of 15 ounce cans or one of the large size cans will give you a good 8 ounces of powder.

To prepare fresh pumpkin cut in half, clean and roast face down on a baking tray for about 50 minutes depending on the size of the pumpkin. Let cool and mash the pumpkin or puree in a food processor.

When the pumpkin puree is completely dry, grind to a powder and pass through a sieve.

Pumpkin powder is very versatile and can be used in many different ways.

Try These Recipe Ideas:

Make your own pumpkin pie mix.

Combine ½ cup of pumpkin powder with the following:

1/2 teaspoon salt, 2 teaspoons cinnamon,
1 teaspoon ground ginger
1/4 teaspoon nutmeg
1/8 teaspoon ground cloves or all-spice
1/8 teaspoon ground cardamom OR 4 teaspoons prepared pumpkin pie spice.

Mix thoroughly and store in an air tight container.

To make pumpkin puree for pie just add 2 cups boiling water to the pumpkin pie mix and set aside to rehydrate for 15-20 minutes. Then use in your recipe just as you would canned pumpkin.

This amount makes one pie. Double the recipe for two pies.

Makes a great gift.

SUPER GREEN POWDER

Kale   Swiss Chard   Spinach

When the garden gives you greens, whether it is kale, spinach, chard or even collard greens, the bounty can be overwhelming. So what can you do with all that green goodness? You can freeze it, of course, or you can make your own powdered supplements. Basically, the process is the same for any of the dark leafy greens.

Preparation:

Wash the greens thoroughly and pat dry. Remove any tough stems and lay leaves on the dehydrator trays in a thin layer. It's important to not overload the trays

Dehydrator temperature: 95°-110°

Leafy greens dry very quickly, so pay close attention.

Greens can also be air dried by laying them out on a tray in a dry area of the kitchen for a week or however long it takes the leaves to dry out. The important thing is to make sure the leaves are completely dry and crunchy to touch, and that they are protected from pests, pets, and klutzy humans.

Once the leaves are thoroughly dry, crush and grind them to a fine powder and pass it through a sieve to remove any hardened stems that may remain.

| Kale | Spinach | Chard |

Use the powders individually, or combine your greens to make your own superfood powder. Put it in everything from soup to smoothies, pasta, and pastry. Make green ravioli or really green goddess salad dressing or even mix with broth, water or formula for baby food. Your imagination is the only limit.

Super Greens Powder

Blend equal parts spinach, chard, kale, or any combination of greens and/or herbs you prefer. You can even mix the greens before drying, then dehydrate and powder them together as a premixed blend.

Powders are shelf stable but should always be stored in an airtight, glass container away from bright light.

Try This Recipe Idea:

Add 1-2 tablespoons powder to <u>Cream Soup Mix</u> (pages 45-46) and prepare as directed.

Put a spoonful in your morning protein shake to add extra nutrients.

SWEET POTATO POWDER

Is it a sweet potato, or is it a yam? Even the supermarket people seem to be confused as well as most of the customers. I like the ones with orange flesh and pinkish to reddish smooth skin. I call them sweet potatoes, but sometimes the supermarket calls them yams.

Sweet and topped with marshmallows, or roasted and savory, it's hard to imagine a holiday dinner without sweet potatoes.

One of the best ways to keep sweet potatoes on hand is to dehydrate and powder them. Whether you call it sweet potato powder, sweet potato flour or homemade instant, you've got the basis for all kinds of quick and delicious side dishes.

Sweet Potato Powder

Preparation:

You can use the same method as pumpkin and cook and puree the sweet potatoes. You can also peel and cube the potatoes, put them on a microwave tray covered with plastic wrap, and microwave the sweet potatoes on high for about 4 minutes. They will be tender but not totally soft.

Transfer cubes or puree to the dehydrator trays, spreading them to allow for efficient drying.

Dehydrator temperature: 120°-135°

When the sweet potatoes are completely dry and crispy, remove from the trays, grind to a fine powder and put through a sieve.

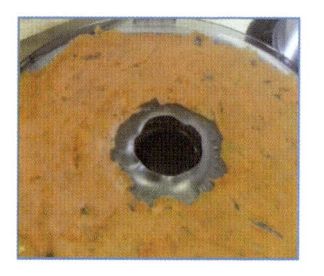

Store in air tight glass container.

Try These Recipe Ideas:

Sprinkle a little sweet potato powder over pet food for a treat and some extra nutrition.

For sweet potato puree, combine ½ cup sweet potato powder with 1 cup warm water and stir until smooth. <u>Let rehydrate for at least 10 minutes and then stir.</u> Reheat in the microwave if needed. Makes a tasty puree for infants.

Sweet Potato Roti

Mix 1/3 cup of sweet potato powder with 2/3 cup warm water, stir and rehydrate for 10 minutes.

Add 1 tablespoon brown sugar, ½ teaspoon cardamom, 2 teaspoons oil, and salt to taste. Combine sweet potato mixture 2 cups whole wheat flour, stir and knead lightly on a well-floured board until soft dough is formed. If too soft to handle, add more flour, if too dry add more water.

Divide the dough into small balls and flatten with your hand. Roll out the dough to desired thinness, turning several times. I don't recommend using a tortilla press as the dough is more fragile than tortillas. Place the roti on a dry hot griddle or frying pan. Cook for 1-2 minutes and flip. Do this several times. The roti should puff slightly after turning. Remove and keep in a basket lined with a kitchen towel or a tortilla server.

TOMATO POWDER

Teach a man to garden and the whole neighborhood gets tomatoes.

Tomato powder is one of the items I use the most in my kitchen. It's the basis for all kinds of basic ingredients: tomato sauce, tomato paste, tomato juice or ketchup. The possible uses are almost endless. It's the perfect solution for using that tomato surplus.

Preparation

There are two ways to make tomato powder. I've used both. The first is to use fresh garden tomatoes, and the second is to use the large #10 can of tomato paste that you can buy at Costco or Sam's Club. I've used both methods.

Tomato Powder

For fresh garden tomatoes, wash and slice the tomatoes and slice about ¼ inch thick. Don't worry about the seeds since you'll be powdering the tomatoes.

For canned paste, spread the paste on your dehydrator sheets (you can also just make your own using parchment paper). Spread the paste evenly.

Dehydrator temperature: 115°-130°

When the tomatoes are dry and crispy, blend to a fine powder and put through a sieve.

When the paste has dried to a stage where you can lift it off the tray, turn it over and continue drying until the paste is dry and crispy.

Blend the dried tomato paste to a fine powder and put through a sieve

Try These Recipes Ideas

Tomato Paste

Mix 6 teaspoons tomato powder with 3/4 cup hot water and stir. Let the mixture rehydrate for 10 minutes. This recipe makes an amount equal to one six ounce can of tomato paste.

Chili

Add 2 tablespoons to your next batch of chili for extra richness and flavor.

Marinara Sauce

Combine 4 cups boiling water with ½ cup tomato powder. Then add the following:

1 tablespoon dried onion
1 ½ teaspoon dried parsley
1 ½ teaspoon dried oregano
1 ½ teaspoon mushroom powder (see pg.25)
1 ½ - 2 teaspoons salt
1 ½ tablespoons garlic powder
¼ cup brown sugar

Simmer until slightly thickened. Add more water if needed.

CREAMY SOUP MIX

One of the secrets to using powders is knowing how to turn powder into something creamy and delicious. Most of us grew up using canned condensed soup in all kinds of dishes from casseroles to gravy. It was convenient but I hated that "canned" taste, so I was really happy when I found the recipe below that can be stored in the pantry. I use it for all kinds of quick cream soups, sauces and gravies.

4 cups dried whole milk*

1 ½ cups cornstarch

½ cup vegan bouillon powder

½ cup onion flakes or minced onion

2 teaspoons celery seed

1 tablespoon garlic powder

1 tablespoon parsley

1 tablespoon Italian seasoning, oregano or herb of your choice

Combine all ingredients and blend to thoroughly mix. Store in an air tight container.

Directions:

In a saucepan, melt 2 tablespoons of butter. Add in the vegetable powder of your choice, and let bloom as you would a spice (this really helps the powder rehydrate and soften). Use 1-2 tablespoons of dried vegetable powder..

Whisk in 1/3 cup soup mix and 2 cups of water to the butter/powder roux. Heat, stirring the mixture until thoroughly combined, and simmer for about 10 minutes or until the mixture begins to thicken. If the soup seems too thick just add a little extra water. You can serve this as a soup, or use as a sauce or in casseroles. These instructions make about 1-2 cups of soup.

Suggested Flavors: Broccoli, Celery, Carrot, Mushroom, Pumpkin, Greens, Sweet Potato, Tomato.

*Dried whole milk can be difficult to find in supermarkets, but you should be able to find it in health food stores or order online. It makes a big difference in the texture of the soup.

FRUIT POWDER

Here are a few points about fruit powder. Fruit powder is delicious, but it doesn't mix well with water and is not a good way to make fruit juice because the texture tends to be grainy. Where fruit powder really shines is in cooked or baked dishes. It's wonderful in salads, as a garnish for fish or vegetable dishes, in hot cereals, and as a base for DIY paints and natural cosmetics.

When making fruit powders it is important to remember that fruit has a higher sugar content than vegetables. This makes fruit powder stickier than vegetable powder so it's a good idea to dehydrate the powder a second or even third time after grinding. Still, fruit powders are well worth the time and effort.

APPLE POWDER

Apple, as well as some other fruits, will turn brown when exposed to air. To maintain appearance dip the fruit pieces in lemon juice, or a commercial ascorbic acid solution.

Preparation:

I like to slice the apples in rings because I find them easier to handle that way but you could also dice them in cubes.

Place the rings on the dehydrator trays in a single layer. You will need to turn the slices several times during the drying process.

Drying time can vary depending on the moisture content of the fruit. The apples are dry when they are bendable but still leathery. At this point you can grind them, but I recommend placing the powder, which will be sticky, back in the dehydrator for another 4 - 6 hours, stirring occasionally to prevent clumping.

Regrind the powder. I sometimes add a teaspoon of arrowroot to the powder to keep it from becoming too sticky. I mainly use apple powder in baking recipes and store the powder, or flour as it is sometimes called, in quart size jars. Depending on the size of the apples, two dozen should be about the right quantity.

Try These Recipe Ideas:

Use apple powder instead of flour next time you make crumble or streusel topping. It's amazing.

Replace ½ cup all-purpose or whole wheat flour with apple flour in your next batch of muffins.

BANANA POWDER

Bananas are probably America's favorite fruit. Unfortunately, they have a very short shelf life and frozen ones are only good in your morning protein shake. So to get that yummy banana flavor even when the banana basket is empty, you can use banana powder as a flavor enhancer.

Preparation:

You should have uniform slices of banana so they will dry at the same rate. I found that my egg slicer was a good solution when working with a large amount of bananas.

To keep the banana slices from oxidizing and turning brown, dip them in lemon juice. Then place the slices on the dehydrator trays, closely but not touching.

Banana Powder

Dehydrator temperature: 120°-135°

Turn the slices half way through the drying process. The chips will be hard and crisp and snap when you break them.

Grind the chips into a fine powder and pass through a sieve. If the powder is still too sticky, put it back in the dehydrator for another hour.

Try These Recipe Ideas:

Stir a spoonful into warm milk and sprinkle with cinnamon for a soothing nighttime snack.

Add to frozen bananas and blend for easy soft serve ice cream to boost flavor.

Replace a portion of the flour in pancakes and muffins with banana powder.

Banana Crepes

1/4 cup banana powder
3/4 cup all-purpose flour
2 large eggs
½ cup milk
½ cup water
2 tablespoons melted butter
¼ teaspoon salt

Place all ingredients into a blender and blend until smooth. Chill in refrigerator before use.

BLACKBERRY/RASPBERRY POWDER

Blackberries and raspberries are antioxidant super stars as well as being delicious. We wait all year for the summer bounty of fresh berries, and in the dead of winter dessert with blackberry or raspberry sauce is a luxurious treat.

Preparation:

The process is the same for dehydrating and powdering both blackberries and raspberries. Rinse and dry the fruit if using fresh berries. For frozen berries just place them on the dehydrator trays unthawed.

Dehydrator temperature: 115°-125°

Blackberry/Raspberry Powder

When the berries are dry they should be firm and crisp.

Grind the berries to a fine powder and pass through a sieve to remove any seeds. Like other fruit powders blackberry powder will tend to get sticky as it settles. Stir the powder frequently to keep it from clumping. Store in an air-tight glass container.

Try These Recipe Ideas:

Use to flavor and add color to baked goods, ice cream, icing and toppings.

Put a tablespoon in your morning smoothie for an extra antioxidant boost.

Add a tablespoon to sugar syrup and reduce to make a quick and easy syrup or berry sauce.

54

BLUEBERRY POWDER

Blueberry powder is the best way I've found to get my daily helping of antioxidant superfood, and it's so versatile that you can find all sorts of ways to use it.

Preparation:

When dehydrating fresh blueberries for powder you can just put them on the dehydrator trays without all the trouble of pricking each one. You can also use frozen blueberries right out of the freezer.

Dehydrator temperature: 120°-135°

Drying blueberries takes some time. These aren't sweet little blueberry raisins. You know they are done when the berries are hard and crunchy.

Blueberry Powder

When the blueberries are dry, grind them to a fine powder and pass through a sieve. The powder may seem a little sticky so you could dry the powder for another hour or two, or add a teaspoon of arrowroot powder to the mix. Store in an air-tight container.

Try These Recipe Ideas:

Mix a teaspoon of powder with a tablespoon of warm water, stir and let rest for 10 minutes. Add to butter cream frosting for spectacular color and flavor.

Sprinkle on top of ice cream and add to shakes for extra nutrition.

Use the powder to make Blueberry Vodka.

Make blueberry sauce without all the sugar.

CITRUS POWDER

Citrus powders are like sunshine in a jar. They not only bring a lot of flavor to all kinds of foods, but lemon in particular makes a great salt substitute.

Preparation:

The powdering process for any citrus fruit is basically the same. Both the peel and the flesh can be dried and powdered. First wash and dry the fruit. With a vegetable peeler, carefully remove the zest from the fruit. Yes, I know some people just dry the whole peel but for outstanding flavor using just the zest is preferable. I use both the zest and the fruit, but for separate kinds of dishes.

Citrus Powders

Whenever possible, I like to air dry the zest. Just place the zest on the dehydrator trays and put the trays in a sunny spot. It takes about 48 hours for the zest to dry. However, you can use the dehydrator on the lowest setting. When the zest is dry it should be crisp when you snap it.

To dry the flesh, remove as much of the pith as you can from the fruit itself, and cut in slices. I use the peeler to remove the top layers of pith. Slice the fruit in ¼ inch slices and place on the dehydrator trays and put in the dehydrator. Turn the slices about half way through the drying process.

When dry, grind the zest and store in an air-tight container. When the fruit slices are dry and crispy, grind them and pass through a sieve to get a fine powder. Store in an air-tight container. Dried orange, lemon and lime powder made from the fruit pulp has a tendency to become sticky and harden. Stir or shake the jar frequently.

The zest is particularly fragrant. Sometimes I open the jar just to enjoy the smell.

Try These Recipe Ideas:

Sprinkle the zest on salad, fish, or vegetables. Lemon is a very good replacement for salt.

Use to brighten sauces, soups and stews.

The powdered pulp can be used to flavor frosting, pastry cream and cookies.

In recipes that call for lemon, lime or orange juice, mix 1-2 tablespoons of powder with lukewarm water.

CRANBERRY POWDER

Most of us only think about cranberries around the fall and winter holidays. But cranberries are great as a secret ingredient, too, and they dry beautifully.

Preparation:

Keep in mind, we are making cranberry POWDER not craisins. There is no sugar involved and the dehydrating/powdering process is different from making the familiar dried fruit. The good news is that it's really easy.

I recommend using fresh cranberries, although you can use the canned to make fruit leather. Give the cranberries a good rinse and drain them in a colander. Put them in a blender or food processor and chop them roughly, just enough to break up the berries. This greatly shortens the time to dehydrate them. Spread the chopped berries on your dehydrator trays. That's all there is to it. Some people like to blanch them so they pop open, but for our purposes here it's really not necessary.

Dehydrator temperature: 125°-135°

When the cranberries have finished dehydrating the pieces should be hard and crispy. Remember, these are not craisins. If the berry pieces are still soft, dehydrate them for a little while longer.

Once the cranberries are dried, grind them and put them through a sieve. Store in an air-tight container.

Try These Recipe Ideas:

1. Add to flour when making muffins or breads.

2. Great added to rubs for meat.

3. Make sorbet, sherbet or ice cream. For quick sorbet, pour ¾ cup very hot water over 1 tablespoon cranberry powder, stir and let rehydrate (about 30 minutes). Add cranberry mixture to ¾ cup sweetened condensed milk. Mix well. Place in shallow container and freeze at least six hours or overnight. Scoop and serve.

STRAWBERRY POWDER

We use strawberries to color and flavor all kinds of foods from soda to cake, so it makes sense to have a supply of strawberry powder to use when strawberries are no longer in season.

Preparation:

You can use fresh strawberries when they are in season, but frozen will also work and it's easier to cut the strawberries when they are frozen.

Place the strawberry pieces or slices on the dehydrator tray in a single layer.

Dehydrator temperature: 120°-135°

The strawberries should be dry and crisp when they are ready.

Grind to a powder and pass through a sieve. Store in an air-tight glass container.

Try These Recipe Ideas:

Add to cake or muffin batter.

Sprinkle on ice cream or hot cereal, or add to yogurt.

Fruit Tea

Mix with warm milk for a soothing before bedtime snack. In a sauce pan, warm 1 cup of milk and 1 teaspoon strawberry powder. Add honey to taste, and stir until the powder has dissolved.

Use to flavor syrups and sauces.

THOUGHTS FROM THE AUTHOR

Thank you for taking the time to read my book. I hope you found it both interesting and helpful.

While there are many other uses for fruit and vegetable powders such as herbal medicine, spiritual practices, cosmetics and more, my purpose in this book was to introduce the concept and techniques of making and using powders. I've included only a few of the vegetable and fruit powders that you can use in your own secret ingredients. I encourage all of you to try this technique and add powders to your own list of secret ingredients.

They will not only enhance your own cooking but they also make great gifts.

Recipe Index

Broccoli Dust 10	Citrus Condiments 58
Cabbage Juices/Soup 14	Cranberry Sorbet 62
Carrot Pudding 16	Strawberry Flavoring 64
Carrot Cashew Hummus 17	Fruit Tea 64
Celery Seasoning/Garnish 20	
Cucumber Seasoning/Garnish 22	
Jalapeno Salt 24	
Jalapeno Chili Paste 24	
Mushroom Soup 27	
Mushroom Gravy 27	
Pumpkin Pie Mix 31	
Super Green Soup 35	
Sweet Potato Roti 39	
Tomato Paste 43	
Chili Sauce 43	
Marinara Sauce 44	
Creamy Soup Mix 45	
Apple Toppings 50	
Banana Crepes 52	
Blackberry Frosting 54	
Blackberry Syrup 54	
Blueberry Frosting 56	

67

Printed in Great Britain
by Amazon